PIANO
Adventures® by Nancy and Randall Faber
Jazz & Blues

This book belongs to: _____

Arranged by

Nancy and Randall Faber

Production Coordinator: Jon Ophoff
Design and Illustration: Terpstra Design, San Francisco
Engraving: Dovetree Productions, Inc.

FABER
PIANO ADVENTURES®
3042 Creek Drive
Ann Arbor, Michigan 48108

A NOTE TO TEACHERS

The **Piano Adventures® Student Choice Series** offers an exciting set of arrangements in a variety of genres and at just the right level of difficulty.

At **Level 2**, the arrangements use primarily 5-finger hand positions for simplicity, yet extend enough beyond Middle C position to reinforce note reading and interval recognition.

Invite your student to choose from additional styles in the series, each arranged at six levels, including:

- Popular
- Christmas
- Classics
- Studio Collection
- Jazz & Blues

Visit **www.PianoAdventures.com**

Die Hefte der Reihe **Student Choice Series** von **Piano Adventures®** bieten anregende Arrangements im passenden Schwierigkeitsgrad und in unterschiedlichen Stilrichtungen.

Stufe 2: Der Einfachheit halber sind die Stücke hauptsächlich in 5-Finger-Lagen notiert. Chromatische Änderungen und Erweiterungen der Lagen fördern das absolute Notenlesen und das Erkennen der Intervalle.

Lassen Sie Ihre Schüler aus den folgenden jeweils in sechs Stufen vorliegenden Heften wählen:

- Popular
- Christmas
- Classics
- Studio Collection
- Jazz & Blues

Besuchen Sie uns: **www.PianoAdventures.de**

De **Piano Adventures® Student Choice Series** bevat fascinerende arrangementen in een keur aan stijlen, precies op het juiste niveau.

In **niveau 2** worden voornamelijk eenvoudige 5-vinger-posities gebruikt, echter niet alleen rondom de centrale C. Dit bevordert het absolute notenlezen en het herkennen van intervallen.

Er zijn arrangementen op 6 verschillende niveaus. Uw leerling kan kiezen uit vele stijlen, waaronder:

- Popular
- Christmas
- Classics
- Studio Collection
- Jazz & Blue

Bezoek ons op **www.PianoAdventures.nl**

La **serie de libros suplementarios "Student Choice"** de **Piano Adventures®** ofrece adaptaciones de piezas cautivadoras en una gran variedad de géneros y niveles de dificultad.

El **Nivel 2** incluye piezas sencillas que usan principalmente posiciones de 5 dedos, pero también se extienden más allá de la posición del DO Central para reforzar la lectura de notas y el reconocimiento de intervalos.

Invite a sus estudiantes a elegir entre los siguientes estilos, cada uno disponible en seis niveles:

- Popular
- Navidad
- Clásicos
- *Studio Collection*
- *Jazz* y *Blues*

Para más información, visite **www.PianoAdventures-es.com**

La serie dei volumi **Student Choice** di **Piano Adventures®** offre una straordinaria gamma di arrangiamenti di diversi generi musicali e livelli di difficoltà.

Al **Livello 2** gli arrangiamenti si basano, per semplicità, principalmente sulla posizione delle cinque dita estendendosi tuttavia oltre la posizione del Do centrale per consolidare la lettura delle note e il riconoscimento degli intervalli.

Invita i tuoi studenti a scegliere tra gli altri stili proposti dalla serie, ognuno dei quali è arrangiato a sei livelli di difficoltà e comprende:

- Pop
- Natale
- Classici
- Studio Collection
- Jazz & Blues

Visita **www.PianoAdventures.it**

IEFF1044

TABLE OF CONTENTS

Jeepers Creepers

Words by
JOHNNY MERCER

Music by
HARRY WARREN

Bright swing

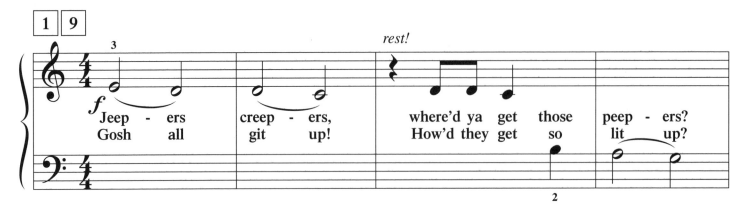

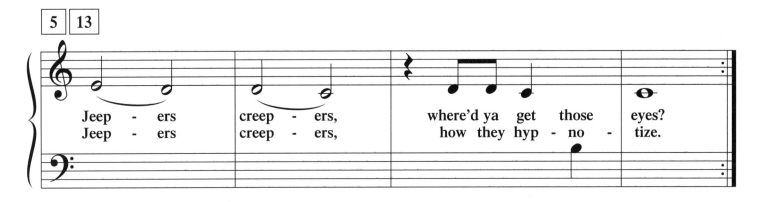

Teacher Duet: (Student plays 1 octave higher)

I'm Always Chasing Rainbows

Words by
JOSEPH McCARTHY

Music by
HARRY CARROL

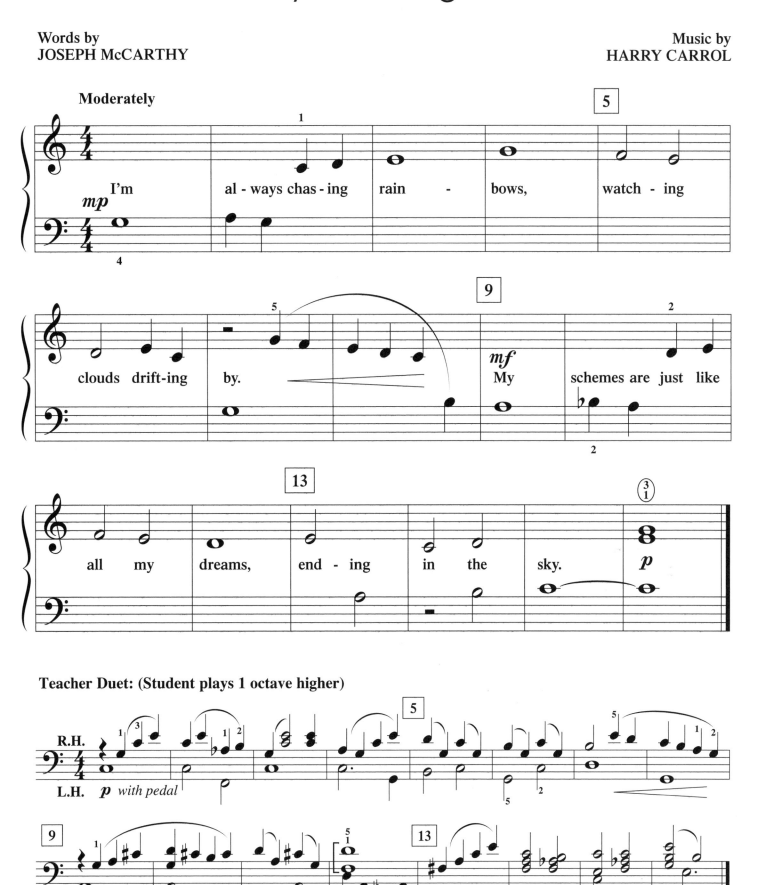

Teacher Duet: (Student plays 1 octave higher)

IEFF1044

Five Foot Two, Eyes of Blue
(Has Anybody Seen My Girl?)

Words by
JOE YOUNG and SAM LEWIS

Music by
RAY HENDERSON

Brightly

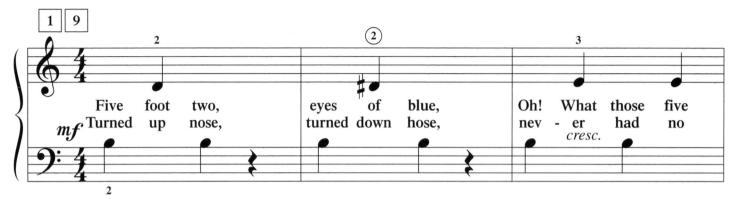

Five foot two, eyes of blue, Oh! What those five
Turned up nose, turned down hose, nev - er had no

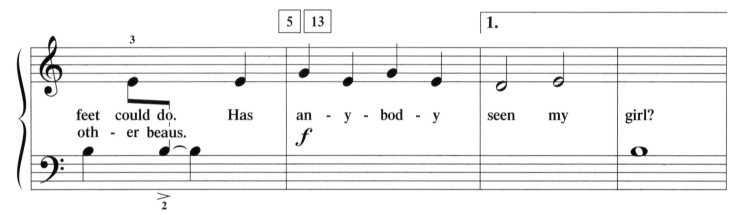

feet could do. Has an - y - bod - y seen my girl?
oth - er beaus.

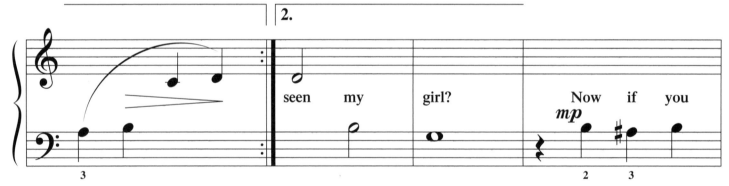

seen my girl? Now if you

Teacher Duet: (Student plays 1 octave higher)

R.H.

L.H.

The Way You Look Tonight

Words by
DOROTHY FIELDS

Music by
JEROME KERN

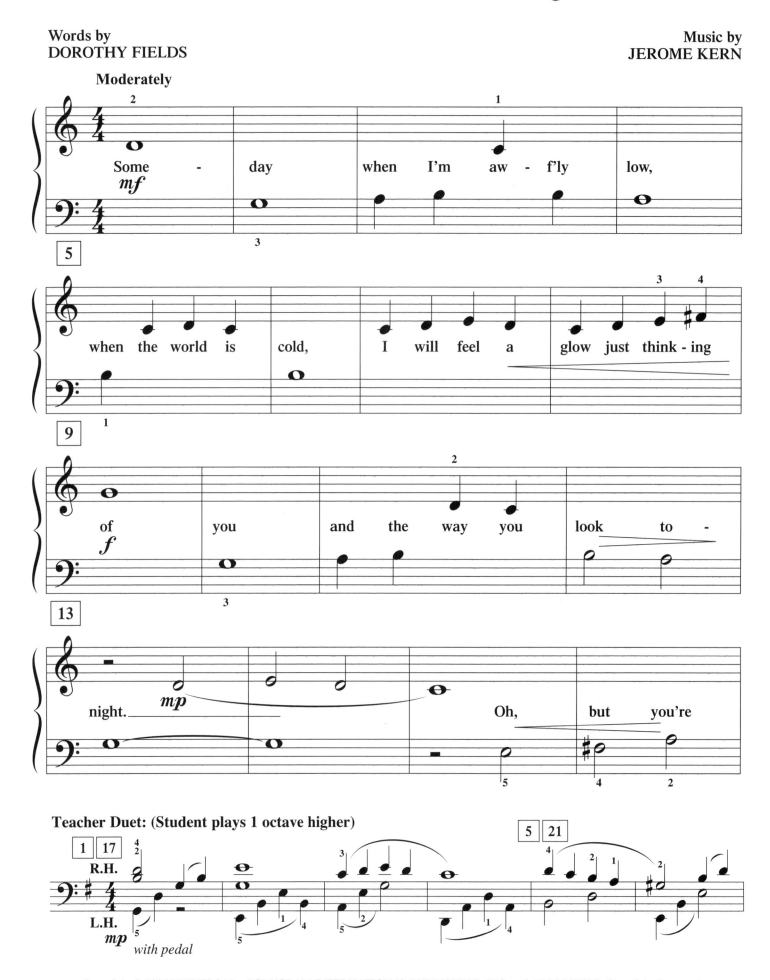

Teacher Duet: (Student plays 1 octave higher)

It's Only a Paper Moon

Lyric by
BILLY ROSE and
E.Y. "YIP" HARBURG

Music by
HAROLD ARLEN

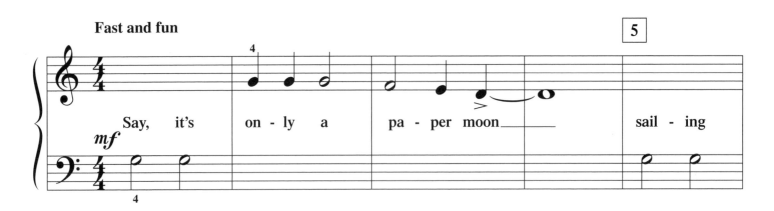

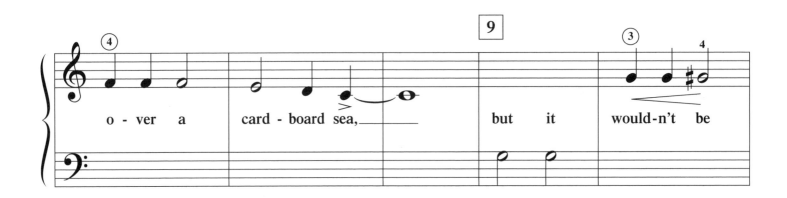

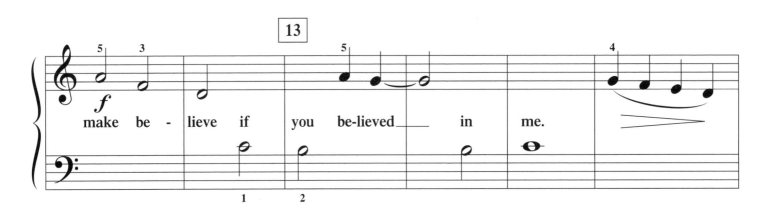

Teacher Duet: (Student plays 1 octave higher)

Yes, it's on - ly a can - vas sky hang - ing

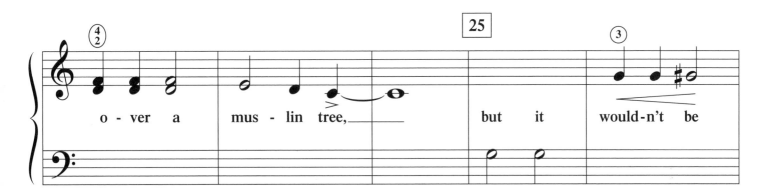

o - ver a mus - lin tree, but it would-n't be

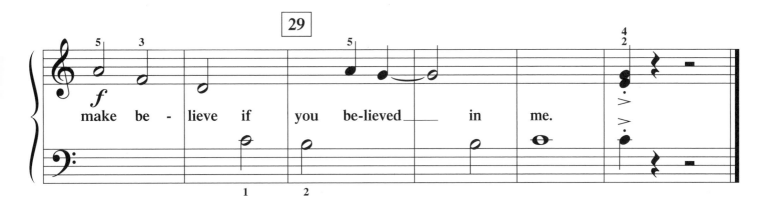

make be - lieve if you be-lieved in me.

IEFF1044

It Don't Mean a Thing If It Ain't Got That Swing

**Words and Music by
DUKE ELLINGTON
and IRVING MILLS**

Teacher Duet: (Student plays 1 octave higher)

Sugarfoot Rag

By NANCY FABER

Happily, no swing

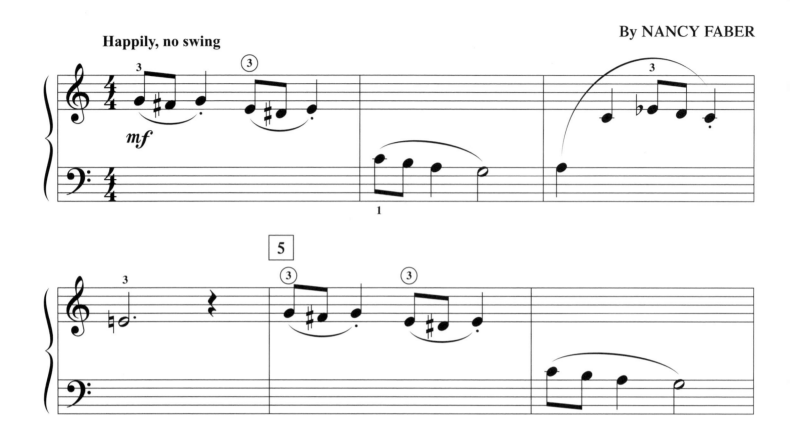

Teacher Duet: (Student plays 2 octaves higher)

Copyright © 1992 Dovetree Productions, Inc. c/o FABER PIANO ADVENTURES.

cross ② over

From the Paramount Picture *BREAKFAST AT TIFFANY'S*

Moon River

Words by JOHNNY MERCER

Music by HENRY MANCINI

Don't Sit Under the Apple Tree
(With Anyone Else But Me)

Words and Music by
LEW BROWN, SAM H. STEPT
and CHARLIE TOBIAS

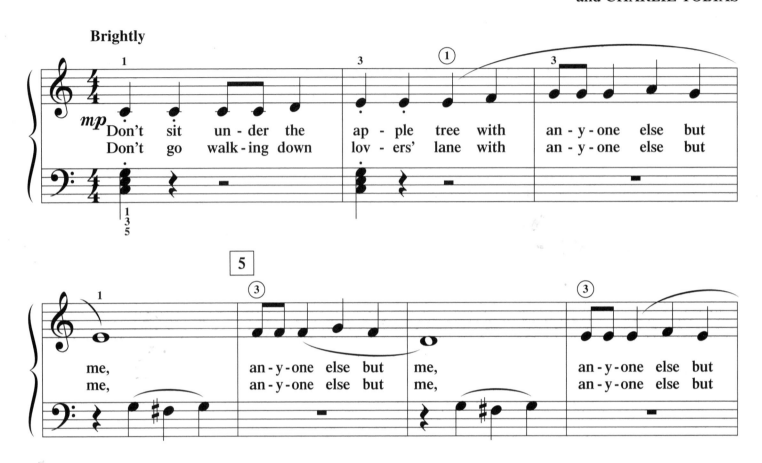

Teacher Duet: (Student plays 1 octave higher)

Ain't She Sweet

Words by JACK YELLEN
Music by MILTON AGER

Teacher Duet: (Student plays 1 octave higher)

Boogie-Woogie Fever

Words and Music by
NANCY FABER

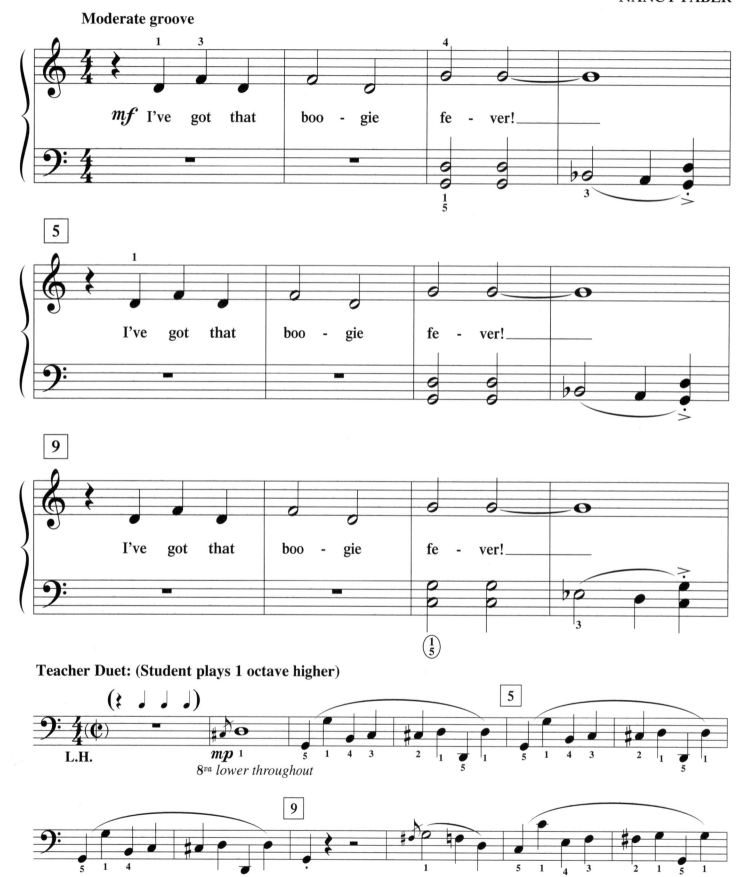

The Blues Monster

Words and Music by
NANCY FABER

With a solid beat (no swing)

as written

Play the lowest
C on the piano!